Master Music Licensing

The 4 Step Plan to Licensing Success

By: Michael Elsner

Copyright © 2019 Michael Elsner

ISBN: 9781098941161

DEDICATION

This book is dedicated to YOU because you've taken the initiative to focus on YOUR music career. I believe EVERY MUSICIAN deserves to be heard, and I'm looking forward to hearing your music on TV very soon!

CONTENTS

INTRODUCTION

Welcome to **Master Music Licensing: The 4 Step Plan To Licensing Success**! My goal is to show you the 4 steps that myself, along with many others, have used to successfully license our music for use in **TV Shows, Commercials, Films, Movie Trailers, Video Games, Corporate Promos, and more**.

To get the ball rolling, I want to give you a CheatSheet that I've created called **The Valuable Content CheatSheet**. It will compliment the information you're about to learn in this book.

GRAB YOUR COPY OF THE VALUABLE CONTENT CHEATSHEET HERE:
https://www.mastermusiclicensing.com/cheatsheet

Now, I disagree whole heartedly with the 'starving artist' mentality. There is no reason why one should have to starve for their art. The best art is created when you're not worried about paying your rent, or where your next meal is going to come from. The best art is created in a world of abundance. One in which the creator has all the tools at their disposal to get their ideas out into the world. One where you have the freedom, and the time, to do it right. The more freedom you have to throw yourself fully into your art, the better the results.

Over the course of my career, I've met incredible artists who've written some of the most amazing music. Sadly, many of them are no longer creating because they couldn't support themselves. Unwilling to change paths, or be open to other avenues of revenue, they simply decided to quit.

The world is missing out on some amazing music right now because these artists had an 'all or nothing' attitude about getting signed to a record label. If they weren't going to get signed, they weren't going to continue to create. So, they moved on in life to a regular 9-5 job in order to keep the bills paid.

You were born a creative individual. **You were meant to create**, not to suppress your gift in favor of a paycheck.

There is a better way. For creative individuals like us, *there is a path to financial security where we can create music full time*, and my goal is to show **_YOU_** that path!

It's one thing to just read about a process verses actually implementing a process. This system works, and I want to encourage you to follow through on each of these steps with your own music catalog.

I wish you much success and many song placements!

"The Price of Anything is the Amount Of Life You Exchange For It"

- Henry David Thoreau

LAYING THE FOUNDATION

The Truth

Let's face it, no one wants to be a starving artist. I haven't met anyone in my career that said they aspired to barely get by in life. Quite the contrary. Every musician I've ever met has dreamt of 'making it big' and living the good life while doing something they absolutely love.

Unfortunately, it's become increasingly more difficult for artists to survive financially as full time musicians when focusing on the traditional paths to stardom and success.

Thankfully, there are avenues that we as musicians can take to achieve the financial freedom we desire while doing what we love - creating music!

It's easy to focus on the traditional paths to success, such as record deals, publishing deals, and touring, but none of those paths guarantee financial success.

The question that I get asked more than any other is, "how can I get my music on TV?" There are weeks where this seems to be a daily question, and to be honest, I've answered it so many times that my response is almost automatic. Since so many musicians have asked me for advice on how I've successfully done this over 2000 times in my career, I wrote this book to show you the 4 Step Process I've used for my own Licensing Success.

The first few questions I ask anyone interested in this field are "What style of music do you write?" "How many tracks are in your catalog?" and "Are you currently working with anyone to administer your catalog?"

Now, I've been fortunate in my career to have written music for over 100 different TV programs, as well as a variety of commercials, video games and film trailers. While this list continues to grow, successfully composing for TV is a world that, to me, has really been quite easy to navigate.

Writing music for these outlets is a very fulfilling endeavor, both financially and creatively. My favorite aspect of writing music for licensing opportunities is that I am fully in control of both my art and career. There's no record label exec, unscrupulous manager, or publisher telling me what to write and record. This creative freedom is what makes licensing music so gratifying.

I believe whole heartedly that anyone can find success pursuing this path. However, as with any successful career, it will require a commitment on your part to follow the steps I've outlined in this book. There is no short cut.

Music Licensing

How often do you hear a particular artist's song on TV shows or movies over and over? Every time you hear that song, licenses had to be negotiated and signed in order to secure the rights to that song for that specific film, TV show, commercial, etc. If you heard that song in two different TV shows, then that process had to be repeated. Every time a song is sync'd to picture of any kind, there must be a signed agreement (ie: license) for that usage.

Definitions

Before we dive into this 4 Step Plan, let's briefly discuss some basic terms and processes that are vital to ensuring your success.

Music Licensing: The process of granting the right to another party for the use of your music.

Master License: The license that is signed by the owner of the recording (the master). Traditionally, if a record label paid for the recording, then the record label owned the 'master.' However, if you paid for your recording, then you own the master.

Sync License: The license that the publisher signs to grant the use of the intellectual property (the song). If you are not signed to a publisher, then you are the publisher.

Master and Sync Fees: The fees that are paid for the use (master and sync licenses) of the song. These fees are generally equal (also known as a Most Favored Nations clause). If a song is licensed for $1000, the Master and the Sync Fees are each $500.

One Stop Shop: This term commonly refers to an individual or company who controls both the master *and* sync rights to a song.

Performing Rights Organization (PRO): In America, this refers to ASCAP, BMI and SESAC. You must be a member of one of these 3 organizations, and they are the avenue through which you will be paid performance royalties. You may only be a member of one of these organizations at any one time in your career.

Royalties: The money that is collected and paid to you by your PRO after the song has appeared on a TV show, radio, film, etc. These are paid quarterly.

Music Supervisor: An individual whose job is to choose the right music for a scene and secure the rights (master & sync licenses) to that music.

Music Library: A company that contracts with composers and songwriters to represent their music to music supervisors. They are a trusted source, have fully vetted all the songs in their catalog, and are a '**one stop shop**', allowing for quick and easy licensing of music. They will take a percentage of the song's income for their services.

Metadata: The information included with/embedded in an audio file. The common metadata that you're used to seeing would be the Artist, Album, and Song Title when you import music into a media player like iTunes. That is only a very small example of the metadata that can be included with an audio file.

Open Your Ears & Listen

So, how profitable can music licensing be? Very profitable. There are many artists and composers who make incredible livings just writing and licensing their music.

Over the next few days, I want you to **listen** to TV. Don't watch it, **just listen**. Listen to the music underscoring your favorite shows. Listen to the music playing through each commercial. When you're online, instead of skipping the promos after 5 seconds, give them a listen all the way through. Just open your ears and listen. There is music all around us, all the time, and a very small percentage of that music is from Top 40 artists.

Someone has to write all that music, and the writers of that music are all generating an income in the form of royalties every time that music is played. Not only that, those songs already generated income when the sync and master licenses were signed.

As you open your ears and listen, you'll notice that there is a never ending stream of opportunity for us as music creators to license our songs for use in TV shows, Films, Commercials, Corporate Promos, Film and Video Game Trailers, etc.

It doesn't matter what genre of music you write, what your instrumentation and lyrical content are, what tempos or production style you prefer to use, there will always be a home for your compositions. Some tracks will find multiple homes, multiple times over. All of this means income for you. The more music you write for your catalog, the more opportunities for placements. The more placements, the more upfront income from licensing fees, and the more backend royalties, often for years to come.

The Sync License

In licensing, whoever controls the copyright (also known as the publisher), controls the right to sync the music to video. In order to sync a particular song to video, a sync license must be negotiated and signed. Since the publisher is the one who controls the copyright, the publisher is the one who negotiates and signs the sync deal.

The Master License

Traditionally, going into a studio and recording an album would cost hundreds of thousands of dollars, so record labels funded the recordings for artists. Once the album was finished, the label owned those particular recordings. They didn't own the songs however. The songs are considered 'intellectual property' that is owned by the songwriter, and controlled by the publisher. The specific recordings of those songs, known as Master Recordings, are owned by the record label or entity that paid for them.

Since technology has made it possible for artists to record incredible sounding projects out of their home studios at very little cost, many artists are now funding their own recordings. This means that they own their Master Recordings.

Understanding These Licenses

In order to sync a song (intellectual property) to picture, the right to sync that piece must be negotiated and granted by the publisher (sync license). The right to sync the specific recording (master license) must be negotiated and granted by whoever owns that recording, also known as the master recording.

Most Favored Nations Clause

So, we now know that in order to sync a piece of music to picture, two licenses must be agreed upon. The sync and the master. The publisher negotiates and signs the sync license, and the owner of the recording negotiates and signs the master license.

Without one, you can't have the other. Meaning, if one of these two parties does not agree to the terms, the deal is off the table.

Enter in "Most Favored Nations." The Most Favored Nations clause is a contractual commitment that states that "no other relevant party will receive better, or more advantageous, terms from the party making the commitment."

Let me show you a real world example of how this works in music licensing deals.

A friend of mine was negotiating a licensing deal on behalf of a film producer for a very well known song that was to be used in a particular scene in the film. He contacted the record label who owned the master recording and they agreed to a $30k master license. When he reached out to the publisher, they wouldn't accept anything under $600k for the sync license. Since the most favored nations clause states that all relevant parties will receive the best agreed upon deal, the record label would now have to receive $600k for the master license even though they agreed to only $30k.

The producer of the film felt the song was worth the $1.2 million it would cost to use it in the scene, and the record label was promptly informed of the good news that they just made $570k more than they were expecting.

The Path To Success

With the basic terms and concepts out of the way, let's talk about generating a solid and consistent cash flow from writing music. If you work diligently, music licensing can be a true path to financial freedom. It's been mine, and I'm going to show you how it can be yours.

Get In The Game

I like to think of my music catalog as an investment portfolio. Follow me on this for a moment. Most financial planners recommend you be diversified, with multiple stocks in different sectors. Basically, this means having investments in the technology sector, a few in the biotech sector, maybe 2 or 3 in the energy sector, and so on. A good investment portfolio will keep you diversified enough through the market's upswings and downturns so that you're always making money.

The exact same thing is true with your music catalog. The more diversified it is, the better. I like diversity, and as a creative individual, I thrive on it. I'm sure the same is true with you.

STEP 1: BUILD YOUR CATALOG

Create Something Today

The very first step in your music licensing career is to start building your catalog. Write as much, and as often, as you can. One or two songs is not a catalog. An album's worth of material is enough to get the ball rolling, but not enough to make a career out of it... yet. It is, however, definitely enough to start opening the doors that will get you on the long-term path to financial success with your music.

If you have the knowledge and skills to produce your own high quality recordings, even better. If you don't, then find co-writers who are skilled producers. The most important thing is to start building your catalog.

Let me give you an example. A few years ago I bought an old 1920's Martin ukulele at an auction. Because I like to put a value on my time, I decided I was going to spend the next two weeks writing and recording 1 new song a day in order to learn how to play the uke. Fortunately, my situation is one where I have a full recording studio in my house, so I have the ability to record my ideas at any time.

For two weeks I learned chords on the ukulele, watched YouTube videos to get some ukulele inspired ideas, and ultimately wrote a new song each day. It was a fun process, and even though I no longer package my material in physical CDs, I still create an album's worth of similar songs before sending them out to my licensing contacts.

As of this writing, that album generated 4 national commercials as well as multiple TV show placements. I was able to generate considerable backend royalties that still come in every 3 months as well as significant upfront licensing fees by simply learning a new instrument, creating some music, and having fun in the process.

It wasn't hard, but it was another project to add to my

diversified music catalog. **Building your catalog** is the first step, and it really is the most important. Your catalog is the source that generates a consistent revenue stream for you. The steps that follow are what allows you to consistently collect and deposit that income into your bank account.

Write Without Boundaries

While we're on the subject of building your catalog, it's very important for me to state this: Don't overthink what you're doing, just have fun and create. It's ok to be in a creative mindset where you're stylistically all over the map. For me, one day I may be writing rock, the next acapella, the next orchestral, the next hawaiian, etc.... I'm not obligated to create in the same genre day after day, and neither are you. At the end of every creative spurt is a period of non-creativity. Those are the days where I take the time to go back through the new material I've written and categorize it.

When I'm done, I may find I have 10 rock tracks, 8 acappella tracks, 7 orchestral tracks, etc. As I stated, I like to organize material into albums before I deliver them to the company that administers my catalog. In this example, I know I have the rock compilation complete, 2 more acappella and 3 more orchestral tracks to write until I have 3 completed 'albums,' or compilations of music, that are licensable. It's at this point that I'll focus on writing and finishing up each compilation.

STEP 2: CREATE VALUABLE CONTENT

...And Then There Were Six

Whether you're writing vocal or instrumental tracks, you can increase your chances of having your music licensed by simply creating multiple versions of each song. If you write vocal songs, make sure to always create an "Instrumental Mix." You may even be able to creatively mute various instruments to create an "Acoustic Mix" or "Stripped Down Mix."

For your instrumental pieces, it will benefit you to create a "No Melody" mix by simply muting the main melodic instrument. As you analyze your main mix, listen for the various other alternate mixes that are possible.

I always like to add in sleigh bells for a 'Holiday Mix.' These are especially popular towards the end of the year, and offer even more value to your catalog.

From one track, you can immediately add 5 or 6 versions to your catalog. Ten songs in your catalog could easily turn into 50 or 60 licensable tracks, depending on how many versions you're able to create, and since each song is different, the number of versions you'll be able to create from each track will be different. The more versions that you're able to create of each song you have, the more possibilities you will have for licensing that song.

GRAB YOUR COPY OF THE VALUABLE CONTENT CHEATSHEET HERE:
https://www.mastermusiclicensing.com/cheatsheet

STEP 3: MASTER METADATA

The Golden Ticket

Now that you've been building your catalog and burning various mixes of each track, what's next? One word: Metadata.

You can have an incredible song that's just perfect for multiple placement situations, but if the music supervisors and editors searching for music can't find your song, then you're out of luck. That's where a solid knowledge of metadata will greatly benefit you.

Metadata is the golden ticket to song placements. This is easily the most important step that you will take to ensure the successful licensing of your material.

Metadata is the information that is included with an audio file, and it allows that song to show up in a search of specific keywords. The best example of this would be your iTunes catalog on your computer. If you open iTunes and you want to listen to a specific artist, you can easily find all their songs in your library by simply typing the artist's name in the iTunes search field. This is an example of metadata in its simplest form.

Sometimes you may notice more information attached to an audio file, such as the album title, composer, copyright year, etc. And sometimes you'll import audio with no metadata, to which it may appear as an untitled song by an unknown artist from an unknown album. That's an example of an audio file with no metadata.

To better understand the importance of metadata, put yourself in the position of a music supervisor for one moment. Let's say that you have over 10,000 songs in your iTunes library, and a producer is asking for a happy, fun, summer, hawaiian-inspired piece that needs to be synced to picture within the next 30 minutes. How would you go about finding options that would fit this request? Are you going to listen to every song in your library? There's no way you'd have the time. Do you have every song in your library memorized? Doubtful.

So, how would you search your music library to find the right song? The first thing you may do is go into your iTunes search bar and start typing in the words, 'happy,' 'summer,' 'hawaiian,' or even 'ukulele.' Any track that has those words included in its metadata will appear in your search. If those words are not included in the metadata, then even the most perfectly suited song will not show up in the search.

Your goal, as a music content creator, is to make sure that your song will always show up in every relevant search. That's the importance of metadata. Simply stated, it doesn't matter how perfect your song may be, if it doesn't show up in the search, it will never get licensed.

In order to get the big placements, it's imperative to master metadata. To do this, listen to your track and write out as many adjectives or descriptive phrases as you can think of. Going with the example above, let's say you've written a happy, feel-good, song with female lyrics and ukulele. Your metadata keywords can be as simple as "Happy, Fun, Upbeat, Cheerful, Summer, Beach, Carefree, Ukulele, Female, Teenage, Freedom, Feel-Good, Laughing, Laughter, Relaxed,"

You should also write out a 1 to 2 sentence detailed description of the song. Don't forget to include the writers, publishers, performing rights organization affiliation, and, most important, the licensor's contact info.

Organization Is Everything

I'm a fan of keeping things extremely organized and simple. In fact, for me, the simpler, the better. I keep a very detailed spreadsheet of every single track I've ever written.

The organization of my columns is as follows: Album

Compilation, Song Title, Version, Writer(s), Publisher(s), Song Length, Tempo (BPM), Category, Sub Category, Song Description, Featured Instrument(s), and Keywords. Some of these are self-explanatory, and some require clarification.

Let me show you the metadata of a track I wrote called Hula. The main instrument is a ukulele, but I also included some glockenspiel, drums, as well as various vocal "oohs" and "ahhs". Along with the full mix, I muted the vocals for a 'No Vox' mix. I also muted all drums and percussion for a 'No Drums' mix. Finally, I added sleigh bells throughout the entire track for a 'Holiday' mix. From 1 master track, I now have 4 licensable versions of "Hula."

Below is my spreadsheet with all the metadata for Hula. Along with the versions, writer and publisher, you will note that Hula is 2:15 is duration, and is 138 bpm. My compilation that includes Hula is titled "Hawaii."

ALBUM	SONG	VERSION	WRITER(S)	PUBLISHER	LENGTH	BPM	CATEGORY	SUBCATEGORY
HAWAII	Hula (Full)	Full	M. Elsner	ME Pub	2:15	138	Hawaiian	Pop, Island
HAWAII	Hula (No Vox)	No Vox	M. Elsner	ME Pub	2:15	138	Hawaiian	Pop, Island
HAWAII	Hula (No Drums)	No Drums	M. Elsner	ME Pub	2:15	138	Hawaiian	Pop, Island
HAWAII	Hula (Holiday)	Holiday	M. Elsner	ME Pub	2:15	138	Hawaiian	Pop, Island

Filling out this spreadsheet takes about 5 to 10 minutes, and I do it while the track is still fresh in my mind. I know all the instruments I used, I know the versions I mixed, and at that point, since the song is fresh in my mind, I can think of a simple, concise description of the track. Finally, under the keywords heading, I think of every possible adjective to describe the track.

DESCRIPTION	FEATURED INSTRUMENT	KEYWORDS
A ukulele driven piece inspired by moments of summer bliss.	Ukulele, Vox, Glockenspiel	fun, upbeat, ukulele, hawaiian, summer, sun, freeing, breezy
A ukulele driven piece inspired by moments of summer bliss.	Ukulele, Glockenspiel	fun, upbeat, ukulele, hawaiian, summer, sun, freeing, breezy
A ukulele driven piece inspired by moments of summer bliss.	Ukulele, Vox, Glockenspiel	fun, upbeat, ukulele, hawaiian, summer, sun, freeing, breezy
A ukulele driven piece inspired by moments of holiday bliss.	Ukulele, Vox, Sleigh Bells	fun, upbeat, ukulele, hawaiian, summer, sun, freeing, breezy

These examples are simplified, but it's not uncommon for

me to think of 30 to 50 keywords used to describe each piece. I generally try to think of creative adjectives that describe the track. Above all, my goal is to make sure that every word that could be used to describe the track is included in the metadata. I do this for every song I write.

You may be thinking, 'why is he putting them in a spreadsheet and not into the audio file?' Well, the answer to that is simple. Depending on who you're delivering your music to (we'll get to that soon), you don't necessarily know yet what file type you have to deliver. Some people prefer AIFF files, others WAV. Some like 24bit/48kHz, while others like 24bit/44.1kHz, or even 16bit/44.1kHz resolutions. Others still just prefer high resolution MP3s. I've learned that it's easiest to catalog each and every track, then when the time comes to deliver them, input the metadata into the files prior to delivery. Plus, I like having a record of every song in my catalog.

Inputting this information onto your audio file is as simple as importing the audio into iTunes or Soundminer, and then filling out the various columns. In iTunes, you can use the Comments column to input the descriptive keywords for each track. Be aware though, WAV files DO NOT store metadata. If you input metadata onto a WAV file, and then send that file to someone, when they import it, no metadata will show up - only the title. For this reason alone, I would advise you to use AIFF or MP3 before wasting your time with WAV files.

Some agencies you work with may even prefer a spreadsheet of the metadata so they can import it into an online resource like SourceAudio. Every time you finish a new track, make sure to add it to your spreadsheet and fill in the columns. It'll make your licensing life much easier in the long run.

STEP 4: GET YOUR MUSIC HEARD

Four Paths

You've been writing and building your catalog, creating multiple versions of each track, and have mastered metadata. The last step is to get it into the right hands. You now have 4 paths you can take to license your music. They are:

1. **Direct to Music Supervisors**
2. **Exclusive Music Libraries**
3. **Non-Exclusive Music Libraries**
4. **Royalty Free Music Libraries**

While all 4 of these paths will lead to licensing success, what I'm particularly focused on in my own career are licenses that pay well. I'd rather license 5 tracks at $10k each, than 100 tracks at $100 each. I'd rather have featured placements on primetime network shows over background placements on infomercials that play at 2am in the morning. I prefer placements that generate both upfront fees and consistent backend royalties.

For that reason, I want to focus on the first two paths.

Direct to Music Supervisors

If you are extremely detailed with your metadata, know the ins and outs of sync and master licenses, are great at marketing, negotiating, networking and building personal relationships, and most importantly, are very prompt at responding to emails and phone calls, then getting your music directly into the hands of music supervisors is the path for you.

There are a significant amount of resources online that contain lists of music supervisors. Every November, "Music Connection" Magazine publishes a directory of music supervisors. It's also advantageous to take advantage of music supervisor panels at various music industry events such as ASCAP's "I Create Music Expo," or South By Southwest (SXSW).

One of my favorite ways of researching who is supervising some of my favorite TV shows is to visit IMDB.com.

Once there, type in the title of the particular show and select the latest season. Scroll down and select "See Full Cast." From here, scroll down to "Series Music Department" and look for the current Music Supervisor.

Researching, and personally connecting with music supervisors, will require you to be creative in your approach. Above all, remember that these individuals have large workloads and are often under extraordinary time crunches. Make sure that your music is something that fits the style of music they're currently using/looking for on the projects they're working on before reaching out.

Exclusive Music Libraries

These deals generally require you to sign your songs with them for a term length determined in your contract. During your contract period, the agency, or music library, may take all, or a percentage of, the publishing for your songs, as well as 50% of all licensing fees. We've all have heard the phrase, "it takes money to make money," and that couldn't be more true in this case.

As my catalog grew, administering it fully on my own to music supervisors became a full time job in and of itself. I found myself spending more time working my catalog than contributing more music to it, which led me down this path. This is a win/win situation, in that by giving up some of my earnings in the form of publishing and sync fees, I make more money simply because I was not able to generate as many weekly licenses administering my catalog on my own.

Just like the music supervisor path, this path requires research and due diligence on your part. Once you have a catalog that you feel is large enough to start pitching, then finding the right exclusive library to partner with is imperative.

Throughout my career, musiclibraryreport.com has been an invaluable resource in finding the right agency to house my catalog with. Over the years I've worked with multiple agencies, each of which came from researching them via Music Library Report, and then actively engaging with employees from each agency.

Signing your catalog with a company should be both a very personal, and very hands on process as this company, and its employees, will be your 'family' for the duration of your contract. Every library has agreements with various networks and production companies. These agreements determine how their licenses work and the opportunities for placement, which are the direct contributing factors to the potential for both upfront licensing fees, and backend royalties.

From a personal perspective, I enjoy the creative freedom of working with an exclusive music library over administering my catalog directly to music supervisors. This allows me the freedom and time to contribute to my catalog as I see fit.

One of the most exciting aspects of this path, for me, is when I check my cue sheets and see new placements that have come in, all while comfortably working away on new material in my studio.

The Others

You can research non-exclusive and royalty free libraries in much the same way. While you can still definitely find success down these paths, there is a definitive difference in the quality of placements and, therefore, financial returns. As I stated earlier, I view my music catalog much like an investment portfolio. I'd rather put my money in an investment that returns 10% annually than ones that return

2%. In my experience, the non-exclusive and royalty free paths are much like the 2% investment, however, the process to house your catalog with either of them is the same as with an exclusive agency.

NOW GO LICENSE YOUR MUSIC!

Frequently Asked Questions

The top 3 questions I get regarding music licensing are:

1. "Who should I send my music to?"
2. "I have a company that wants to represent my song, but I don't want to give up my publishing."
3. "What's the difference between a Music Library and a Music Supervisor?"

I get asked this first question more than anything else. The hardest step for most people is the 4th step - getting their music directly into the hands of music supervisors and music libraries. However, this isn't nearly as difficult as you may think. Doing your research, and tailoring your pitch, goes a very long way.

This process is covered in great detail in the Master Music Licensing Course. Presenting yourself as a Valuable Service is imperative to your success, and in the online course you will master my **Bulletproof 6 Step Approach** to successfully contacting & delivering your music to music supervisors and music libraries.

Above all, I want to encourage you to start adopting a mindset of abundance. Just listen to TV for a few days, and you will realize there is an abundance of opportunities out there for your music! However, you MUST take the initiative, and follow these steps in order to get your music licensed.

Question: I have a company that wants to represent my song, but I don't want to give up my publishing.

Answer: I say this all the time, "50% of something is better than 100% of nothing." Do you have the industry contacts to get your songs out to the right people in order to generate income? Do you have great negotiating skills? Do you understand contracts? Will you be able to generate the most income possible for each placement request?

If you can't honestly answer yes to each of these questions, then you would greatly benefit from having a publisher or signing with a library.

You have to give someone the incentive to work your music for you, and if you're not going to give them any financial incentive, then believe me, they're not going to spend the time and energy working your music.

If you want to have success, and generate revenue from your music, then you will generally always have to give up something along the way. Remember, 50% of something is much better than 100% of nothing.

However, before you go signing away your rights to your publishing, make sure that your contract states (1) a *term-limit*, and (2) a *reversion clause*. Navigating your way through licensing contracts is another topic discussed in depth in the Master Music Licensing Course.

Question: What's the difference between a Music Library and a Music Supervisor?

Answer: A Music Supervisor is an individual who works with the producer and director of a project to find the perfect song for a scene. The goal is always to get the most emotional impact out of a scene with the ideal marriage of imagery, dialog, and music.

Sometimes, while putting together a scene, an editor may throw in a piece of music from a popular artist that fits just perfectly. The music supervisor's job is then to either secure the sync and master licenses to that particular song, or to find a better, more fitting song at a lower price.

Sync and Master licenses for a hit song from a major artist can cost in the hundreds of thousands of dollars. If there is a limited budget on a production, the music supervisor's job is to find and license a song that captures the emotional impact of the scene perfectly, all the while negotiating a lower rate than a major artist's song would cost.

This is where the independent musician's songs thrive. Instead of licensing an Aerosmith song for $100k, a music supervisor may license your song for $10k.

FINAL THOUGHTS

The idea of knowing that millions of people are hearing your songs every day, AND you're making a living from it, is not just a crazy dream. It is the reality for many musicians, and it can be your reality as well!

I hope this short guide has inspired you, and opened your eyes to the various avenues available for licensing your music, as well as the potential for your own success in this industry.

This 4 Step process has allowed me to generate over 2000 placements of my own music in TV, Film, Commercials, Video Games, and Movie Trailers. There's nothing like upfront sync fees, as well as recurring 'mailbox money' in the form of royalties, to keep a consistent stream of income coming your way.

Licensing your music allows one to not only avoid the typical starving artist route, but to actually make a great living while at the same time allowing financial, personal, and creative freedom. I wish you the greatest success and look forward to hearing your music on TV very soon!

GRAB YOUR COPY OF THE VALUABLE CONTENT CHEATSHEET HERE:
https://www.mastermusiclicensing.com/cheatsheet

ABOUT THE AUTHOR

I'm Michael Elsner and I'm a guitarist, songwriter and producer with over 2000 placements of original music on TV Shows, Films, Commercials, Video Game & Movie Trailers, and more. My tracks have appeared on over 700 episodes of over 100 different TV shows including American Idol, The Voice, Amish Mafia, EXTRA, The Sing Off and So You Think You Can Dance.

Through my premier trailer music company SonicTremor, I've written music for Film and Video Game Trailers including Disney's Cinderella, Ocean's 8, The Condemned 2, Dragon's Dogma, Endwar, as well as a Super Bowl Commercial for Amazon Prime's Jack Ryan Series.

Over the years I've spoken on the topic of music licensing at numerous music conferences, and after talking with so many struggling and starving musicians, I realized there was a lack of actionable resources available to empower musicians to **THRIVE** *in the modern music industry. To answer that need, I created a number of* **In-Depth Online Resources:**

- **Master Music Licensing**
- **Real Musicians Don't Starve**
- **The Song Placement Workshop**

Each of which is available at:
www.MasterMusicLicensing.com

For a current list of credits, visit:
www.MichaelElsner.com

Made in the USA
Monee, IL
12 April 2021

65547659R00017

Have you ever dreamed of having your music featured in TV Shows, Films, and Commercials?

Wouldn't it be amazing to know that millions of people are hearing your songs every day, AND you're able to make a great living from it?

This is more than just a dream. It's a reality for many musicians, and it can be your reality as well!

Successfully licensing your songs is a MUST if you want to survive in the Modern Music Industry, and this book details the 4 Steps necessary to generate consistent placements.

By implementing this 4 Step Plan, you will save years of trial-and-error, and get on the Fast Track to Licensing Success!

About The Author:
With over 2000 placements of original music in TV Shows, Films, and Commercials, some of which include American Idol, The Voice, EXTRA, The Ellen DeGeneres Show, Disney's Cinderella, Amazon Prime's Jack Ryan Series, and Oceans 8, Michael Elsner has mastered the art of sync licensing by implementing this 4 Step Plan that you are holding in your hands right now.

ISBN 9781098941161

90000

9 781098 941161

WHY OUR **Children** WILL BE **Atheists**

The last 100 Years of Religion and the Dawn of a **World without Gods**

Albert Williams